A Forest in His Pocket

poems by

Ray Cicetti

Finishing Line Press
Georgetown, Kentucky

A Forest in His Pocket

This book is dedicated to all my teachers, especially
Robert Jinsen Kennedy, S.J, Roshi
who with great love introduced me to myself.

ACKNOWLEDGMENTS

Grateful acknowledgment to the publishers of the following journals and
books (some in earlier forms with different titles)

Exit 13 Poetry Journal, Issue 24, 2019: "Climbing South Twin Mountain"
The Metaworker Online Journal October 2017: A Forest in His Pocket
(formerly, "Coming Home")
Tiferet Journal Spring/Summer 2018: Alone in a Restaurant (formerly "The
World Soul")
Tiferet Journal Fall 2018: "Japanese Cherry" received an award in the
Carriage House poetry contest,2018
Tiferet Journal Spring/Summer 2019: "Nuthatch"
Special thanks to my wife Carolyn whose love and support are a constant,
to Adele "do you really need that word" Kenny for her editing skills and
guidance, and Carl Bachmann and Vic Carlson for their encouragement and
friendship.

Publisher: Leah Huete de Maines
Editor: Christen Kincaid
Cover Art: Jeffrey Beauchamp
Author Photo: Jeffrey Beauchamp
Cover Design: Elizabeth Maines McCleavy

Printed in the USA on acid-free paper.
Order online: www.finishinglinepress.com
also available on amazon.com

Author inquiries and mail orders:
Finishing Line Press
P. O. Box 1626
Georgetown, Kentucky 40324
U. S. A.

Table of Contents

I

II

III

I.

Shame on you, Shakyamuni
for setting the precedent of leaving home.
Did you think it was not there—
In your wife's lovely face
In your baby's laughter?
Did you think you had to go elsewhere to find it?
—J. Collins

ARRIVING
(for Ritchie)

He was the Lenny Bruce of our 8th grade class, Brylcreem hair, sharkskin pants, white socks when we all wore black. His tie was as crooked as mine was straight, but he was nobody's fool. The nuns put him at the back of the class. They called him trouble, we called him cool.

He knew how to fight and smoke and wonder. When Sister Rose pointed to the photo of the five soldiers who raised the flag on Iwo Jima, as the only ones left. He asked, Who took the picture?

He asked: *if Mary had a virgin birth, wasn't she a single mom? Why do we never hear about Jesus and his dad? And, if Lucifer means the bringer of light, what light does he bring?*

His questions pulled me from the pocket of my innocence. The nuns hit him hard though he told me his father hit harder, when he was around.

But after he fought a teacher over his essays on how God allowed the Viet Nam war, and blacks to be beaten in Birmingham, I never saw Ritchie again. And my classmates whispered, *Elvis has left the building.* There was a hole in the class that year. I loosened my tie and began to wonder.

WAKING UP IN BELMAR NEW JERSEY

I was just a boy when
on that sandy slope in August '63
I looked up into the midnight sky
and realized the insanity of stars,
the magic of blue meteors
that screamed across
night's immense body
and lifted me into mystery.
How what I always thought was mine
dissolved like smoke in that magnetic air
my name on fire, forgotten,
launched into something
I could not know.

JAPANESE CHERRY

He never wanted (even as a boy) wings to fly like other boys, or like a superhero to punch through walls when he could walk around them. Once, he thought about being a star so he could shine each night, but changed his mind, for what was the point of stars except to see their light. No, he always dreamt this is how it could be, to stand in a tree's long journey. New growth around and through him, translucent white blooms from every branch. Here, he catches the wind, knows the rhythm of rain—head straight into the sky, feet rooted in the earth. And he gives shade to those who need it, limbs for children to climb.

A FOREST IN HIS POCKET

Once there was a man who found a forest in his pocket. When he came home after a day's work he took it out. His house would fill up with deer and bear, green moss, amber grass. He strolled through green valleys and stands of old oak that poked through his roof into the sky. He cooled his feet in a flowing stream. He rested in the clear air as he ate his dinner. His neighbors came out to hear to the sound of birdsong and rushing rivers. On occasion, people gathered on his lawn drawn by the call of the forest. Even those who came to complain, once inside wanted to stay. He invited them in for a meal, shared stories into the night. And they gazed with wonder at blue mountains, constellations in the sky, and began to remember their true names.

IMPERMANENCE

I'm happy in my lounge chair
this cold spring morning,
double espresso in one hand
meditation book in the other.
On the radio, the Stones play
Time is On My Side, which
the Buddhists now tell me
is not true. Time is not on my side
but an endless stream of instants,
like unseen fingers that flip through
our lives.
Would I want it different?
Would I want love to stay the same?
To possess it?
Or to live in perpetual grief
for those now gone?
How would it be if the jasmine didn't flower,
or the ripe pear didn't fall?
What if the cherry blossoms across the yard
never flew from their branches
to color the bare ground?

LAST NIGHT

Just before death's frosty wing
passed over my father's bed
he lifted his arms toward me
as if he wanted to fly
or to somehow embrace
the undiscovered.
Perhaps, I thought, to say the things
he never said to me.

He was quiet and true
what he thought and felt well kept
behind the papers he read
(the New York Times, the Daily News)
while I wandered the streets

Still that last night
out of love or fear
I do not know—he wrapped
his withered hand around mine
and in that moment,
everything was alright.

He and I like two poles
that life swings between.
He to be made whole
by what he knew,
I to be made whole
by what I do not.

MY FATHER'S VISIT

I sit down to write a poem about a "blue moon"
when my father's ghost shows up.
Hand on my shoulder he says
so, you're writing poetry now?

The day flips backward.

Rarely did he ever ask me what mattered.
We didn't speak much during his last few years.
But here he was, in his old brown jacket
head tilted as he leaned in, curious,
with gentleness in his voice.

MY MOTHER'S SPIRIT

MY MOTHER'S SPIRIT comes to visit me as I make marinara sauce for dinner. I feel her hand on mine as I stir the pot, then her wispy voice "try a bit more salt." I start to move aside to let her take over but she is reluctant. Maybe there is some contract among the dead not to mingle too much with the living. We sit down to chat about unfinished things. How she worried that I kept a distance with others like my father. How I set the family on fire when I left. She says she has forgiven me for that. She tells me it is safe to ask for help, asks if I made peace with my brother. Her face is illuminated and open; judgment absent from her words.

I think to myself she has found liberation in death. I tell her I miss her. I ask how it is being dead. Is she in heaven or some cloud like realm? She whispers, *there is only eternal stillness that for the living is a blink of an eye. Keep your heart open,* she says, and is gone.

MY DEAD GRANDMOTHER ROSA MAKES A VISIT

They were telling that story again
at the dinner table—
how like stone she was—
when she pulled up a chair.

I was surprised she looked so content
her face like the sunny port of Naples
her hair sea foam white.
My mother, lips pursed, ignored her
my father, her son, astonished at the sight.

I asked if grandpa was with her.
Yes, she said, *happy in a lounge chair
above the earth's cold surface.*

I never really knew her.
Then her warm hand touched mine
and she became a spray of flowers.
Their yellow scent filled the room,
and like a phrase of particles she
disappeared into the perfumed air.

INSPIRATION

There is no such thing as writers block,
you just have to lower your standards.
—W. Stafford

I'm up before dawn to write only to realize I can't find my inspiration. I usually leave it under my pillow or on the nightstand. So, I seek it out in the usual places, the flowering jasmine, Miles Davis' *Kind of Blue.* I sit under some old oaks, listen hard for inspiration's music through their leaves, but feel only an impatient chill. Nothing works, my day a crumpled piece of paper.

I return to my desk, pen in hand and stare out the tall window, but the world has a hard edge. There's only my grumpy neighbor with his damn barking dog, a jogger who shows off his smooth stride as he glides by. I peruse books that tell me to breathe, clear my mind, focus on one thing. I light a candle, burn incense, sit cross-legged to meditate. But I can only think about new furniture, how to get more Democrats elected, what pasta dish I'll make for dinner. And all the while, the sunlight shimmies and shines as it slides across the floor.

JUKEBOX

In a dream I am a jukebox, all lit up, pulsing colors of gold and green. My head a blue neon arc, my feet shining metal wheels. And my chest, a window filled with racks of 45's. People stop me on the street, and want to hear their favorite tunes, some from long ago. I watch them smile and sway as they listen-and remember-new love, longing, and loss. "Autumn Leaves" gets a lot of play as does Elvis's "Love Me Tender." "Stardust" is a big hit and Joni Mitchell's "Case of You."
When I roll into town on summer nights, children gather. They dance and sing in circles around me. Some just want to push my buttons but I don't mind.

Golden leaves fall,
Our favorite song plays—
Where are you?

ABOVE THE TREELINE AT LONESOME LAKE

Dawn sunlight moved,
ephemeral and cool across Mount Lafayette
when the buffed pine warbler
close in the low barberry,
launched his ferocious song like an arrow
over the empty boulders
and I recalled my old teacher's words
the particular transcends the general.

I know the world is on fire,
I know days pass like sunset's blaze—
how we walk blindly
toward our dream
of some other Jerusalem.
But now on this mountain edge
I don't care about other days,
what may or may not come.
I am held in the warbler's
yellow song that rings out now
over the green mountains
without *if* or *when* or *why.*

A MAN SITS ALONE BY THE WILLAMETTE RIVER

Where she used to sit
now only dew and dried leaves.
Sad water lilies float in the grey water.
The man sits next to himself.
His dreams slouch by a tree.
The song of his body drifts underwater.
The river feels his grief.
It knows how things come and go,
how time evaporates.
It assembles itself to sit with him,
puts one silky arm around him,
enters him like sunlight.
The man becomes a vessel.
He sets out on the water,
oars trembling through morning fog.

II.

The most beautiful thing we can experience is the mysterious.
It is the source of all true art.
—Albert Einstein

WHEN GANDHI IS YOUR ROOMMATE

You usually find him in meditation, or spinning cotton on his little wheel. He's so quiet you hardly know he's home. When you forget to clean up, he takes care of it. With a gentle pat on your shoulder he reminds you, *it is the quality of our work, which will please God and free us, not the quantity.* You apologize and promise to do better.

On Sunday afternoons he's in the living room negotiating peace with your Jewish and Muslim neighbors. You feel guilty when, on the street he stops to talk with every homeless person. You fiddle for change as he listens to their stories of hardship and struggle. When you ask why he cares so much he replies, *the best way to find yourself is to lose yourself in service to others.*

He is not perfect by any means. He embarrasses you when friends stop by and he is only wearing a loincloth and shawl or talks endlessly about his famous salt march.

After he invites your girlfriend to sleep with him, you ask him to move out. He tells you it was only to test his vow of celibacy. When he asks you to forgive him, you hesitate; then, he reminds you that forgiveness is an attribute of the strong. Somehow you want to apologize, and promise to do better.

HOW THE UNIVERSE BEGAN

It's life Captain, but not as we know it.
—Mr. Spock

It did not begin with the Big Bang or random molecules connecting in primordial ooze, but with six Italian men playing bocce ball in a park one cool summer evening.

In the Beginning, they stood at the edge of the court and talked about soccer, who lost money at poker, the new deli in town, and politics in the neighborhood. The staccato rhythms of their words echoed out, gave shape to the void, and shook the stars into being.

And when they rolled the pallino down the empty court, time began and the moon and the sun appeared. And all the bocce balls tossed became planets, collided with other planets, and found their places in the universe. And when their work was done, they went to the first café, spoke about what they had made, sipped espresso from little cups, and said it was good.

HALLOWEEN PARADE

Women stopped jogging on their treadmills, men put down their weights to look, when a box of Crayola crayons led her pre-school class in a procession through the gym. A ninja warrior led the line, followed by princess Leia, who kept a wary eye on a hobo in baggy pants who wandered off to beg for candy. Wonder Woman strode in with her golden lasso, at her side a zombie who looked lost, as zombies are apt to feel. Superman stumbled on his red cape, which is understandable when you first take on a new identity. And a yellow butterfly, wings open, flew from the back of the line to hold hands with a freckled faced daisy. If you ask why this made me think about what matters, I have no answer.

CLIMBING SOUTH TWIN MOUNTAIN

We hop-jump on moss-covered rocks after a night of hard rain. Morning sun slants through patches of goldenrod, mountain laurel. As we ascend Vic points out spruce and fir, the air touched with a scent of decay, evergreen. By mid-afternoon we drop our packs, slump down, swig good scotch from a silver flask. Rub aching toes. We feast on noodles, sausage and cheese then nestle into a silence that only exists above tree line.

I stand at the cliffs edge where the blue valley curves like a blade through the Franconia and Willey range. My thoughts turn to Ta-Lung, that old Zen monk who wandered for years through his mountain refuge. How he answered a young monk's question about the eternal by showing him the colors of mountain flowers and valley streams. I drink cool water from an old tin cup. I can see for miles through the mountain air.

THE BUDDHA IN MY HOUSE

*When a woman is a Buddha, she already has virtue
that illuminates the ten directions.*

—Dogen

The Buddha in my house knows comfort
wears a pink robe and slippers,
no sackcloth and sandals for her.

The Buddha in my house is musical
you might hear her sing "Maria"
or "Porgy I'm Your Woman Now."

The Buddha in my house knows patience
unless I forget to feed the birds
or put the garbage out.

The Buddha in my house is virtuous,
hands held out to the haunted and lost;
her mantra, "the same daylight lives in us all."

The Buddha in my house knows
generosity, how the cup
receives the tea without complaint.

The Buddha in my house is wise,
she doesn't look to satisfy every desire,
she knows what we seek is in our hands.

The Buddha in my house is forgetful,
leaves her tea cup on the counter,
last year's Christmas lights on the ground.

The Buddha in my house is fierce in love—
over and over she willingly enters
the dragon's cave for me.

THE RED COUCH

It was a cold Thanksgiving Day
when we hiked,
happy through the woods,
watched the speckled hawk soar,
almost invisible through the shaded sky,
then returned home
content in our time
where I lay down, slept
then woke, when you slid
the curved slip of your body
behind mine—
your breasts pressed against my back
the half-moon of your cheek
nestled into the nape of my neck
like so long ago, in my apartment
in Belleville New Jersey
where (cherry trees in bloom)
we held tight to passion's thread,
the memory vivid now
even as it falls away
on this red couch
as we lay together in the dry air,
your autumn hand on my chest.

SPRING MORNING

I wake from a deep sleep, walk into the kitchen where she hands me coffee, then the curved arc of her embrace, her warm lips.

I thought I knew what love was, I have said it is pain, it is pleasure. But now, on this spring morning there is only the fragrance of sleep in her hair, and something unknowable that does not seem to move even as it passes.

I WATCH THE OLD COUPLE

I WATCH THE OLD COUPLE cross the street as if crossing a stream. She, unsteady on her walker, he, one hand under her elbow, the other on his cane. From a nearby bench a young woman looks up from her phone, watches them before she returns to examine the polish on her fingers and toes. The old woman watches, smiles toward the ground, the man picks up the pace, his face tightens in concentration. They no longer look ahead or behind as they go to the other side. They are of one body now. They know the world is unstable and round.

I WOKE UP THIS MORNING TO A WREN'S SONG

I WOKE UP THIS MORNING TO A WREN'S SONG, insistent and clear in new light, a symphony of sound that rang out from her little brown body over neatly mowed lawns into my room.

I felt like a boy again on the first day of summer when time was an ocean and days had no name or number. And though I move more slowly now, hair grey or gone—every paradise lost. For a moment I was new again, spring (feathered and green) flew from my window.

III.

The Great Way has no gate. A thousand paths lead to it.
—Lao Tzu

PRAYER

I heard on the tail of the breeze this morning that the mountains, rivers and animals are conspiring to re-take the earth so we will stop to remember the forgotten places beyond our vanities and know again the calls of robin and wren, the untranslatable language of oceans. Perhaps then, the morning's blue pastures will sing their songs again and we, forgetting ourselves may find our way back home and recall our own original shining.

ALONE IN THE RESTAURANT

ALONE IN THE RESTAURANT, I turn to an article about how we all share a world soul that runs through everything, doesn't come or go but shows up moment after moment as compassion, some essential connection, or that ocean-like swell in the chest at the sight of a sunrise, death, or a new born child.

I look up from my magazine curious about this possibility to see an inebriated man refused another drink by the bartender. I watch two Hispanic wait staff, invisible to most, laugh with patrons as they clear dirty plates and glasses from empty tables.

At the far end of the room, my waiter in his starched white shirt and bow tie now offers a young couple, unhappy with their meals, new ones for free. My heart lights up like a struck match when he lifts his head, turns toward me and smiles, as if responding to something we both know, some invisible thread between us, so obvious it doesn't have a name and no one even thinks about it.

LETTER FROM A MOUNTAIN POET: SUMMER

Not many know the way here, only those who are lost or broken. You must come. In the deepest part of these mountains there's an endless field. Distant high peaks stand like elders that blend into a single whiteness. Wildflowers sweep sorrow's field. Here, my thoughts dissolve into the high air. Not many know the way here, only those who are lost or broken. The day is a choir. The mountains sing me awake, or perhaps I sing the mountains awake—I'm no longer sure. On the summit I lean into moments of freedom. When I descend, the world appears again. Up and down I walk until dust and freedom are the same. The way to enter is from the west, over dry riverbeds, through thickets and brambles until you say "yes" without knowing why.

LETTER FROM A MOUNTAIN POET: AUTUMN

Autumn arrives on the west wind. Red-orange leaves fire through spruce and fir over the backs of hunched rocks. In the distance, mountain peaks rise like empty buildings. They stand in watch above green shadows that stretch across the valley. And the day has become more of itself though there is less of it. The air is still as the cap in my hand (the one you gave me so long ago).

At night I sit alone by the fire. My only visitors, two gray jays that share my meal, and one pale star on the horizon. My life opens its eyes and looks at me. Will I ever see you again?

LETTER FROM A MOUNTAIN POET: WINTER

A snowstorm rushed in from the west yesterday, more than a foot down by dusk. It made prisoners of spruce and maples, stole the land's contours. I walk from the house and step past myself into groundlessness. The nearby meadow is a single hue, only a few boulders stand up in protest. A branch cracks and two crows flap up, they send down a flurry of snowflakes. In primal silence, a half-moon hangs behind cloud light. Before the first word—a primeval silence touches me.

LETTER FROM A MOUNTAIN POET: SPRING

After three days of hard rain, the storms have passed and the sky is a blue mirror. Even the birds' dark songs lighten in this new air. Today, as I climbed a twisted mountain trail something arrived, simpler than thought, like some clearing without shadow. Before and after fell into something intimate even as the moment changed—direct like an impatient kiss. And some part of me unfolded. I could walk again through the green world; touch the boulders' open chests, free as sunlight through the unknown day. There was bird song, there was music.

GARDEN BUDDHA

Of the statues around our home, the garden Buddha is my favorite.
He's the salt of the earth, molded from gypsum, water and sand. He's
so serene, as he looks out from his grassy seat. Even when blue jays
squawk and fight from the low branches, or squirrels come too close
and do their squirrely dances.

Like me, he suffers embarrassment and indignities. Chipmunks eat
nuts on his lap then leave empty shells. The troubled boy next door, in
a fit of anger, knocked off his head, how it lay like a stone all winter, on
the bare flowerbed.

He is not caught up in the certainty of eye, or images of mind. He
looks beyond the importance of beauty, the unknowable rush of time.
Some days like a trickster, he disappears into the green world, though
he never goes far. And how content he remains, wishing nothing else,
when I get fussy, and move him around the yard.

MR. JONES SOLVES HIS KOAN

How do you stop a flying bird?

—Zen Koan

His body stands him up from the park bench.
He argues but his body wins.
He walks himself out into open meadow,
Sniffs the blue air,
Launches into empty sky from coiled knees,
Becomes flight,
Remembers life is movement,
Becomes movement,
Bends around corners of endless sky,
Sees his dream-self below,
Turns and turns,
Becomes sky.

THE FIRST DAY OF MY RETIREMENT

The October sun shines this morning, gleams off the yellow mums happy in their brown beds.

Drivers honk and shout on their way to wherever they're headed, while I sit inside this café, newspaper in hand, and sip espresso from a little porcelain cup. I won't be in my black leather chair to listen and offer insights to clients today. No longer will I be an interior designer for other people's lives.

Maybe it was because of summer days, scotch in hand, Bill Evans on the radio riffing out *Lucky to Be Me*. Or the many hikes under a green canopy, refreshed by mountain air.

Not even today's front-page news about the increase of depression and stress can sway me to hang my shingle out again. There is a young couple at the end of the café arguing. I hope someone will tell them love is a river. How it arrives in unfamiliar ways. When they give me a sideways glance, I offer a nod of understanding, then call the waiter for another espresso, and open the paper to the sports section.

I WAKE UP MY HOUSE

I WAKE UP MY HOUSE, swig some espresso, jump into the car, and put the top down. I shift and turn in wingless wonder past blue-brown woods. Silver leaves stagger down like happy drunks. Birds' dark bodies sing from the trees. Jubilant streets join hands. Autumn drops its number. The day is a prophet. The sparrow's song is a temple bell. Four women laugh on the other side of a café window. I must remember this.

NUTHATCH

I watch it fly across the yard, carrying sunrise on its back, then land upside down on the sugar maple, wings tucked in like a teaching, only to disappear into the dark woods, like a small blue god's visitation. How I want to follow it, praise it, cup its soft fierceness in my hands.

I step into the moment, arms outstretched, and secretly become a bird. I breathe in autumn's fullness and turn in the crisp air.

The morning lifts me like wings over charcoal roofs. I warm my lined face with my hands, far away from the poverty of knowing. Awake as I will ever be.

CPSIA information can be obtained
at www.ICGtesting.com
Printed in the USA
BVHW030244140421
604817BV00006B/352